1 Children of the poor on an outing organized by the Birmingham
Clarion Cinderella Club (founded 1893), 1901

2 *(overleaf)* Coming in from and going out to the suburbs for the cost of 1d all
the way: horse buses from Balsall Heath in Station Street on a windy day in
high summer. The date is *c.* 1893

*Victorian and Edwardian*

# BIRMINGHAM

*from old photographs*

*Introduction and commentaries by*

DOROTHY McCULLA

B. T. BATSFORD LTD
LONDON

First published 1973
Reprinted 1974, 1985
First paperback edition 1978
Text © Dorothy McCulla 1973
ISBN 0 7134 0128 1

Printed and bound in Great Britain by
Anchor Brendon Ltd, Tiptree, Essex
for the Publishers B. T. Batsford Ltd
4 Fitzhardinge Street, London W1H 0AH

**3**  In Arden, now called Dolphin, Lane, Acock's Green, *c.* 1900

# CONTENTS

# ACKNOWLEDGMENTS

I would like to thank the following for their kind permission to use photographs from their collections: Birmingham Reference Library, Collection of Photographs (4, 7, 9–15, 17, 19, 20–3, 25–33, 35, 37, 39–40, 42–3, 45–6, 48–56, 58, 60–3, 68, 70–2, 76–7, 79–88, 90–3, 95, 98, 100–1, 103, 105–6, 111–13, 115–17, 119, 122, 125, 130–4, 139, 144, 146, 148); Birmingham Reference Library, Sir Benjamin Stone Collection (16, 47, 65–7, 69, 73, 75, 78, 102, 108, 135–8, 140–1, 145); Birmingham Public Works Department, Photographic Section (6, 8); Birmingham Museum and Art Gallery Collection (99, 147); Cadbury Ltd (126–9); John Marks for glass lantern slides (2, 18, 57, 59, 114, 118); Gerhard P. Schienke (96–7); John Whybrow Ltd (24, 44, 89, 94, 110, 142). I would also like to thank Mr W. G. Belsher for rephotographing much of the material appearing here.

D.M.

**4** Life in poster form on Saturday Bridge in Summer Row, August 1901. It is said that the bridge took its name from the men who waited there, each saturday, to be paid

# INTRODUCTION

*Wherever man is, there is Birmingham:* the slogan of the Victorian age. Yet a passenger on the Liverpool to Birmingham railway in the summer of 1837 would have looked across the rolling landscape to see 'the mighty workshop of the World' nestling amid gardens of great beauty in the leafy county of Warwickshire.

The government of the town at this time is best summed up in the words of the *Birmingham Journal*: 'We have our Court Leet and our Bailiffs chosen by themselves; our Town Commissioners chosen by themselves; working in the dark, unseen by the public eye, irresponsible to the public voice; appointing their own officers, levying taxes at their pleasure and distributing them without check or control as their inclinations shall determine'. Although the Reform act of 1832 created Birmingham a parliamentary borough the crowning dignity of a municipal charter of incorporation was lacking. However, steps were taken in March 1837 to obtain the important charter and finally on 6 March 1838 the *Birmingham Journal* was pleased to announce that Queen Victoria had granted the Charter of Incorporation. The first town council was elected on Wednesday 26 December 1838. It must be recorded that much confusion surrounded the arrival by rail from London of the actual document to the town. After abortive visits to the railway station (later called Curzon Street station) the agitated collector was told that it had, most probably, gone to Belfast by mistake!

In 1841 Birmingham was described as 'one of the most extensive manufacturing towns in England'. Most major towns in the kingdom seem to have been dominated by one industry and the prosperity of the town depended on the expansion or the depression of that one industry, for example stockings at Leicester, and cotton in Manchester, but Birmingham in the 1840s boasted of some 500 distinct manufactures. The directories of the period reveal that each industry was divided into several branches so that well over 2000 trades were carried on, linked in some measure but independent of each other in their manufacture. This infinite variety which gave elasticity to the trade of Birmingham also gave each workman an aptitude of thought and action which enabled him in turn to apply initiative and invention to change his occupation in times of stress or to convert a dying trade. Each modest factory employed only a small number of workers. Many of the employers worked or had worked at the factory bench themselves, therefore the gap between master and man was not wide. Each could remain an individualist, sturdy and independent, both working together side by side with mutual respect. Most of the employers were Nonconformists or descended from sober industrious Nonconformist stock. In consequence the style of living of the wealthy citizens was simple, comfortable and not given to ostentation. In many cases the small factory and the dwelling house of the employer stood side by side and it was customary for the employer's wife to quietly look after the welfare of the workers as well as assisting with the business.

Due mainly to its elevated site, the health of Birmingham compared favourably with other large English towns at the beginning of the Victorian period. Even today in this age of pollution, it is possible to find oneself suddenly refreshed by a strong fresh breeze blowing across the face of the City. Most of the streets were macadamised and paved with Yorkshire stone. It is recorded that they were kept clean by Mr Whitworth's sweeping machines, and these were 12 in number. Each year in March, 23 water carts commenced to water the streets. The artisans often lived in separate dwellings enclosed in squares or courts. These courts were the main feature of the town's housing heritage as some were built in the eighteenth century. Providing the courts were laid out on sufficient ground to admit fresh air, with paved surface areas and the dwellings within, well constructed and attached to the water supply, town life was quite pleasant. Unhappily only a small area of the town was attached to the water supply and as the century advanced many of the courts were laid out on small areas of badly drained land. Often the buildings were so crowded together that the air and sunlight failed to penetrate the gloom. Unhappily, all the slaughter houses of the town were situated within the badly drained courts. In consequence by the year 1849 the once healthy town was reported to be unwholesome in parts. To make conditions worse these already crowded areas of squalid dwellings and noisy little workshops had to accommodate the rapidly expanding population. Even Hagley Road carried along with it an open sewer until improvements were made in 1852, and Brass-house Passage was known to be the worse-drained place in the town. A very unhappy man during this period must have been Mr J. Bliss, Inspector of Nuisances!

A map of 1825 shows Birmingham as a town of small gardens elaborately designed and planted with fir trees. These gardens were massed on either side of Garrison Lane at the north side of Ashted Row to the great public garden of Vauxhall. They stretched northwards from the General hospital to Aston Park and westwards across to Lozells farm and southwards down to Sots Hole which could now be identified with the corner of Somerset Road and Edgbaston Park Road. The design details of one garden were not recorded on the map but the words 'refused admittance', substituted instead, seem to reflect some opposition to the survey. It is amusing to imagine the scene between a stubborn landowner and an indignant surveyor, who committed his feelings to posterity when he had the words 'refused admittance' printed on the map. Unhappily, before the middle of the century was reached, some of the most beautiful of the private gardens in the town and the allotment gardens had been swept away, although many remained until the 1880s. Landowners on the outskirts of the town let their gardens, popularly known as the guinea gardens, for 21 shillings per year to artisans in search of peace and tranquility and where they could grow food for their families. From watercolours of the period it seems that as the gardens became scarcer, more plants seemed to appear on the window-ledges of houses and workshops. Horticultural societies increased and numerous shows were held in the area. Most of the taverns on the outskirts of the town also possessed tea gardens where the tired worker and his family from the dark court and unventilated workshop could enjoy gardens and flowers and other rural delights of the period, including boxing matches. Birmingham was then known to be the centre of provincial pugilism. The Angel Inn at Sparkbrook was a popular meeting place for the family at this time.

Excursions by rail were a pleasant form of enjoyment for those who could afford trips to London at 19 shillings return. Some 100,000 people travelled from Birmingham to London to the Great Exhibition of 1851, which is believed to have been modelled on the Birmingham Exhibition of 1849.

Choral music has always been a popular recreation in the town, indeed it was on the sunny morning of 26 August 1846 from the Birmingham Town Hall, that Mendelssohn 'gave Elija' to the world. During the century the Musical Festivals held a dominant position among the recreations of the town and several musical associations were established. In March 1847 twopenny concerts for the people were advertised. The most famous theatre was the Theatre Royal in New Street, but the demand for the popular amusement of the music hall grew as the nineteenth century advanced. At first the public houses provided this form of entertainment, particularly the Old Rodney in Coleshill Street and an establishment of James Day in Smallbrook Street. In 1846 Holder's Concert Hall took the place of the Old Rodney and James Day built the Crystal Palace Concert Hall in 1862.

Public parks were established to replace in some measure the old tea gardens but the tradition was still carried on in the Aston Lower grounds, where the inhabitants of Birmingham and Aston spent leisure hours looking at firework displays, circuses, melodramas, cricket and aquariums or just admiring flowers, while others enjoyed the thrills of skating, boating or boxing, but towards the end of the century the lower grounds became less popular. Few people know that in 1864 Major Gem and Mr Perera were playing a new game on a smooth lawn in the garden of a house called 'Fairlight' in Ampton Road, Edgbaston: the game now known to the world as lawn tennis! Public football grounds were established on the outskirts of the town and brought forth some excellent players.

Permission to hold the first fair in Birmingham was granted by Henry III in the year 1250. Unhappily the great Whitsuntide and Michaelmas fairs which were still held in the Bull Ring area became too popular and so disrupted the life of the town that the Council abolished them in 1875.

Ultimately it was the preparations necessary for the building of the two great railway stations, New Street and Snow Hill, which cleared away a considerable portion of slum property and brought about the rebuilding of Birmingham in the

1850s. The process continued throughout the 1860s when many small work-shops, shops and houses were demolished in the Colmore Row area, after the Colmore estate leases expired; although most of the professional men of Birmingham still lived around St Philip's churchyard and Newhall Street. In 1870 Edmund Street was reconstructed and as the 'seventies advanced the old dwellings and shops in Ann Street and Colmore Row were torn down and the street area widened to enable the Council House buildings to be erected. Indeed many of the old shabby, overcrowded, humble, but multi-purpose cottages which at one and the same time served as homes, shops and factories were replaced by fine palatial buildings; as Eliezer Edwards observed: 'Nowadays we go to a palace to cash a cheque.' Indeed it could rightly be said that the remark still applies to Birmingham in the present year.

The modest bow-shaped windows of tiny stores gave way to monster plate-glass windows of fine shops and 'establishments of quality'. Nearly one thousand trees were planted in the main streets to transform the town. To attempt to assess, with some degree of accuracy, the land values of the period would be difficult, but land at the corner of Worcester Street and New Street was bought by the Town Council for £53-10s-0d per yard.

In the year 1874 the mayor of Birmingham, Mr Joseph Chamberlain, took steps to obtain for the town control of the gas supply from the Birmingham Gas Light and Coke Company and the water supply from the Waterworks Company. He realised also the necessity for another main thoroughfare from the centre, to the north-eastern district of the town. The cutting of the new road would inexorably wipe away an evil-smelling area, packed with common lodging-houses, slums which had festered around the Old Square and Lichfield Street. The Council approved the scheme in 1875 and the cutting of Corporation Street began in August 1878.

As the century advanced, shopping arcades were built. They are still remembered with affection by the older generation who recall with nostalgia the intangible spirit of each arcade. The young wives of yesterday talk of happy meetings with friends from distant suburbs for afternoon tea and cream buns, served on a balcony above the Birmingham Dairy Company. The average factory girl, however, had to buy her new clothing through factory clubs. For example, if 15 girls wanted to purchase boots they would agree to pay 6d each for 15 weeks. Lots were drawn each pay day and the fortunate winner of the week would take the 7/6 to purchase her boots or whatever item of clothing was involved. She usually breakfasted on bread, lard and tea and rarely ate fruit and vegetables. For entertainment she spent 2d per week on a visit to the music hall and a 1d a week into a girls' club for drill or sewing lessons. Sixpence a week was put aside for the Easter outing. Much personal heroism must have been involved in trying to keep respectable!

The Acock's Green and Balsall Heath estates were sold in building lots in August 1839, but it was during the middle of the century that business men and prosperous artisans, either from the desire to further business interests or to seek fresh air, started to build themselves modest dwellings with small gardens in the suburbs. Undoubtedly some factory owners, keen to speculate, merely followed the railway line until they found a convenient place nearby to build a factory. As the outward flow of inhabitants persisted, so horse omnibuses endeavoured to link the new areas of settlement. In 1868 the General Omnibus Company started services from High Street to all the suburbs: the commuter age had definitely begun.

In 1873 a tramway worked by horses was opened from Colmore Row to Handsworth. Narrow-guage lines were constructed in the 1880s and steam was adopted in 1882, closely followed by cable and electric traction. As well as the electric tram, it must be recorded that the year 1889 brought city status to the town.

The story began with a Victorian town and it ends now with an Edwardian city, whose population spread beyond the boundary to increase and strain the resources of neighbouring villages to create suburbs. Indeed Erdington was the first suburb to realise the administrative advantages of a greater Birmingham scheme. The city met great opposition from local councils who protested and fought unification, but the Bill passed through the Lords on 19 May 1911. At last the city and suburbs were united to bring together people and to span 13 miles.

# SETTING THE SCENE

**5** Tram officials waiting in the mist outside the Junction Inn, Francis Street. It is hard to believe that Vauxhall Gardens, reputedly one of the finest places of recreation outside London was, until 1850, just a few yards away

**6**  The castellated building in the photograph was known in the eighteenth century as Allins Cabinet of Curiosities (a general clothing store), or the Flag, because the Union Jack could usually be seen floating from the parapet. In the nineteenth century the building became Bryan's pastry shop and was patronised by Town Hall audiences. The property was demolished when the Council House was built, May 1867

**7** Ann Street: the site of the Council House. The bronze statue of Sir Robert Peel, the work of Peter Hollins, unveiled on 27 August 1855 was the subject of a Victorian joke: 'Why is the Town Hall like an orange?' 'Because it has Peel outside'. The statue now stands outside the Police Training College, Pershore Road, c. 1871

**8** Another view of Ann Street, looking towards the Town Hall, May 1867. The land for the Council House was purchased for £33,000 in 1853

**9** The new Council House in Council House Square, later renamed Victoria Square, *c.* 1880. The foundation stone was laid on 17 June 1874. To commemorate the event the Mayor gave a luncheon at the Great Western Hotel, Monmouth Street, which was followed by a display of fireworks in Aston Park. The first meeting of the Council chamber took place on 9 November 1878

**10** Paradise Street, showing the Midland Institute on the left with Christ Church in the background, *c.* 1889. The foundation stone of the Midland Institute was laid by the Prince Consort on 22 November 1855. To this building came the workers eager to extend their education after the few years of school life they were then allowed. The Earl of Dartmouth, acting for King George III, laid the foundation stone of Christ Church on 22 July 1805. It was the first church in Birmingham to have free seating for the public, but the sexes were separated. This gave rise to the following epigram:

*The churches in general we everywhere find*
*Are places where men to the women are joined;*
*But at Christ Church it seems they are more cruel-hearted,*
*For men and their wives are brought here to be parted.*

**11** The Belle Vue Temperance Hotel, which was demolished in 1905, can be seen behind the memorial. The photograph, it was recorded, was taken at 11.00 a.m. in April 1904

12 Moore's Oyster Rooms, New Street, formerly at the foot of Christ Church, 1890s

13 *(overleaf)* The Chamberlain memorial, inaugurated 26 October 1880. The photograph shows the Reference Library on the left, with Mason's College, Edmund Street, later the University of Birmingham, behind the memorial. The date is about 1900

**14** *(left)*  Corbett's Temperance Hotel and Joe Hillman's dining rooms at the top of Pinfold Street and Hill Street: the site of the present Post Office (which in turn is due for demolition). It has been recorded that the ancient custom known as the Sweeps May Day, a degenerate relic of Morris dancing, centred around Pinfold Street, where at one time most of the sweeps of the town lived, June 1887

**15** *(below, left)*  Another view of Corbett's Temperance Hotel. The sign on the building next-door, No. 6, reads as follows: 'The London Hatters, hats cleaned and blocked while you wait', June 1887

**16** *(below)*  The same site, but the photograph shows the Post Office during the course of erection, which commenced in 1889. Business started on 3 August 1891. Taken from the Town Hall about 1890

17 The demolition of Christ Church started January 1899: the last few loads

18   Newhall Street on a sunny day in the Nineties

19   An accumulator car introduced in Suffolk Street on 24 July 1890 to run to Bourneville. The date is about 1900

**20** *(left)* Shopping in the Midland and City Arcades, *c.* 1905

**21** *(right)* This building, which was completed in 1829, was the exhibition hall of the Society of Arts. The portico was allowed to extend across the pavement to enable visitors to remain dry when alighting from their carriages, 1902

**22** *(below)* This street was known as New Street in the fifteenth century but this was how it looked in 1902

**25**　Station Street at the turn of century

**26** *(right)*　No. 29 High Street, nearly opposite the junction with New Street, in 1900. The fine rainwater-head bears the date 1687. The building was demolished in 1902–3

**23** *(top left)*　The Central Station, New Street, about 1900. Here was the centre of railway traffic, the lines belonging to the London and North Western, the Midland and Stour Valley and South Staffordshire. The roof, which rested upon 45 doric columns, was composed of 100,000 feet of iron sheeting some 1,400 tons in weight. It was constructed by Messrs Fox, Henderson and Co. The entrance to the Queen's Hotel can be seen at the middle right of picture

**24** *(left)*　In this picture of New Street Station the indicator points to the Walsall Express, in the days when one could hire a rug or pillow for 6d. (*c.* 1905)

**27** A leisurely ride across the Bull Ring while the clock on St Martin's church stands at ten minutes before two. Within, the Lords of Birmingham sleep in their tombs while the market they started, sometime between the years 1154 and 1166, lives on in this photograph. (*c.* 1883)

**28** A rear view of the Market Hall, in Worcester Street, about 1900. This building, which was designed by Charles Edge at a cost of £67,261, was opened in November 1834

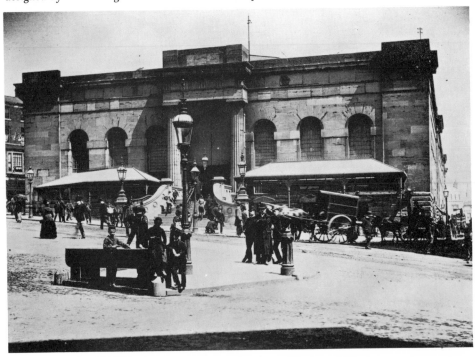

**29** *(right)* Conversation piece at the feet of Lord Nelson in the Bull Ring monument was unveiled on 25 October 1809. (Turn of century: platina

**30** A load of straw being weighed by the Birmingham Weights and Measures department on the Smithfield cart machine in Jamaica Row, *c.* 1890

**31** *(left)* Precinct shopping at the beginning of the twentieth century in the City Arcade, which was erected in 1902. A quick cup of tea and then back home to the suburbs by horse bus! (*c.* 1903)

**32** The day of the Hospital Saturday, or Workmen's Collection, which was made for the free benefit of all the medical charities in the town, *c.* 1893. This photograph is of Corporation Street, the thoroughfare that came into being in August, 1878

33 This busy thoroughfare, now called Steelhouse Lane, was once Priors Conygree Lane (i.e. the rabbit warren of the Priory of St Thomas the Apostle). Gifts to the Priory commenced in the year 1286, c. 1906

34 Snow Hill Railway Station, opened in 1852, as the Birmingham and Oxford (Great Western) railway terminal. The building was erected in 1870 while the photograph was taken in 1913

35    At the corner of Great Hampton Row and Wells Street in 1901

# PEOPLE

36  Newspaper vendor in Lower Tower Street, January 1905.
His poster tells of the Russian defeat at Port Arthur

37 Court No. 1, Thomas Street: typical of the miserable conditions swept away by the great improvement scheme of Mr Joseph Chamberlain. The photograph dates from about 1871

38 Birmingham Express Motor 'bus – Milnes Daimler outside the Council House, Colmore Row, 1904

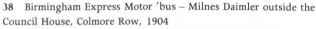

39 (right)   Soon to be re-housed: these women toiled away at home industries, helped by t children. This photograph was taken about 1872 at the back of Nos 12 and 13 Upper Priory

**40–42** 'Children of the Poor' (the description supplied by the photographer) photographed in Sutton Park during the summer outing provided for them by the Birmingham Cinderella Club, *c.* 1898

**43** Children of Birmingham in the year 1898

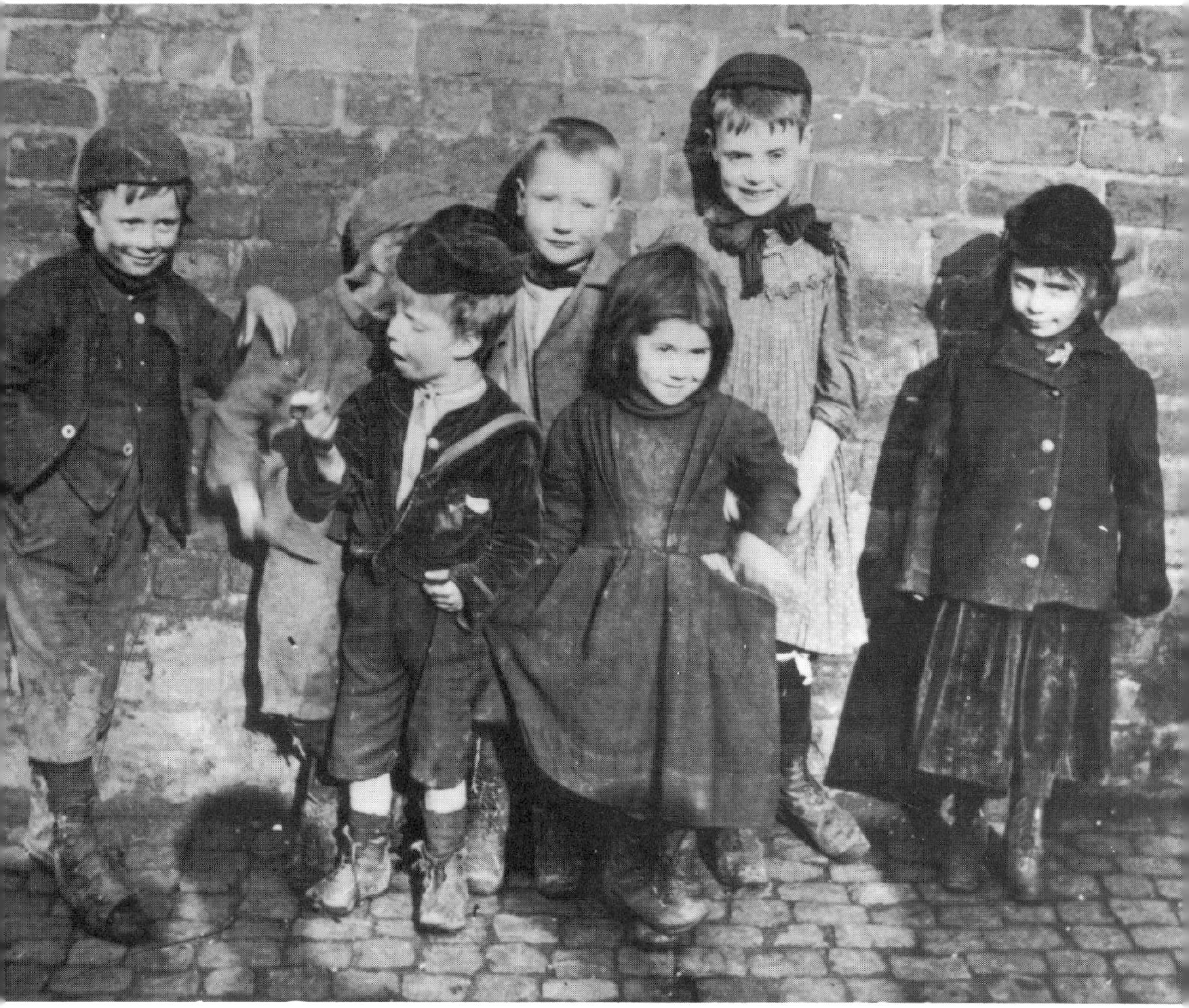

**44**   Court No. 3, Victoria Courts, 1905. From a print made through the back of the negative

**45**   Little patients with the Matron and nurses at the Royal Orthopaedic Hospital, Newhall Street, 1897. An Orthopaedic Hospital was first established in Birmingham in the year 1817

**46** Collecting material in connection with the Science Teaching System, Birmingham Board Schools. The time was 11 a.m.; the date October 1891. It is interesting to note that the science demonstrator to the Birmingham School Board was the man responsible for the photograph, W. Jerome Harrison, a noted geologist

47   Afternoon tea at the Grange, the home of Sir Benjamin Stone, in July 1899

# MARKETS
# AND STREET TRADERS

**48** The water-cress seller trying to keep her goods fresh in the open market in Moat Row. The date recorded by the photographer is 18 June 1901 at 11 a.m.

**49** The flower market in the Bull Ring. The photographer noted on the back of the print that the street lamps were lighted with incandescent mantle and gas. The picture, he further recorded, was taken between 11 a.m. and 12 a.m. on Thursday 31 October 1901

**50**  Italian women buying onions at the corner of Moat Row and Jamaica Row. The date is 1 June 1901 and the photograph was taken by a Hand Camera (quarter plate)

51    Waiting outside the fish market in the Bull Ring, *c.* 1885

52    Flower sellers in the Bull Ring, *c.* 1900

**53** Outside the Market Hall. The older generation recall the occasions when Mr Mountford, the butcher, often had to defend his wife and himself with his own butcher's knife from 'thugs', when he sold meat off cheaply to the poor on Saturday nights, 1901

**54** Customers arriving at the dining stalls inside the Market Hall, 1901

**55**  In the Fish Market, 1901

**56**  Fish and game stalls situated in the north avenue of the Market Hall, 1901

**57** Looking for bargains at the open market in Moat Row, *c.* 1901

**58** *(below)* Like the previous picture, this one is of a corner of the Horse Market (later enclosed to build an extension for the covered market). The photograph is a bromide enlargement from Hand Camera negative and was taken on 20 July 1901

59   Arriving at the market, *c.* 1900

60   At the Horse Fair in Bristol Street on 26 September 1901. The first Horse Fair was held here in 1777; the thoroughfare was then called Brickiln Lane

61    Herb merchants and Neapolitan violet sellers at the corner of Phillips Street and High Street in July 1896

62   This boy, described by the photographer as a street scavenger, is working in Paradise Street. At this period Paradise Street still retained the original wooden pavement laid in 1875. Street orderly bins were provided for such pavements, together with granite for the collection of horse and other refuse. The date is August 1903

63  *(overleaf)*  Lavender sellers in the Bull Ring. The lavender was sold in penny packets. The picture was taken on Thursday morning of 18 July 1901

# THE WORKSHOP
# OF THE WORLD

**64** The photograph of an unknown 'smith'; an archetype of industrial Birmingham, *c.* 1895

**65** Rag sorters at the paper mills, Landor Street, 1895

**67** The usual morning scene in the mill yard, at the Union paper mills Saltley. The mills belong to Smith Stone and Knight, June 1895

66    The office staff of the Union Mills, June 1895

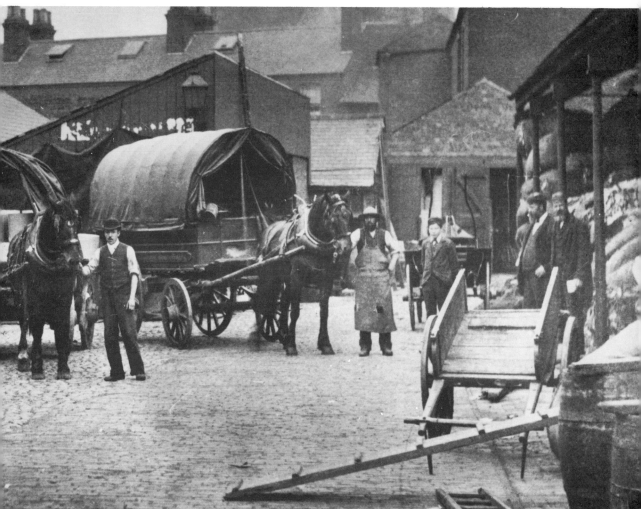

**68** *(left)* A scene in Regent Row: a typical example of Birmingham's infinite variety of small workshops. The following trades were crammed together in this narrow passage: paperbox maker, gas fitting manufacturer, press tool makers, brass founders, coal merchant, jewellery and glass cutters, lapidary, crate makers. The photograph dates from about 1900

**69** *(right)* Duddeston flour mill, kept by Mr Robert Evans, miller, 1864

**70** Iron bedsteads being packed for shipment, 1902

**71** Bedstead manufacture: punching and studding angles at Fisher, Brown & Bayley's works, Lionel Street, 1902

**72** Inside the old mill in Fazeley Street, 1893

**73** The visit of His Imperial Highness Prince Tsai Tse, cousin of the Emperor of China, and members of the Chinese Special Commission to the Metropolitan Railway Carriage and Wagon Company, Saltley. As a result of this visit 30 cars were ordered for the Shanghai and Nankin Railway. The date is 14 May 1906

**74**  Midland Canal Scene. The seamen and Boatmen's Friend Society was established in 1846 to bring the Gospel and schooling to the Canal people and also to provide shelter for canal horses, *c.* 1911

# GREAT OCCASIONS

75　Electors at Nechells Green listening to the Address of the Home
Secretary, the Rt Hon F. Matthews, during the East Birmingham
Parliamentary Election, 1892

**76** The foundation stone of the new church of St Cyprian, Hay Mills being laid by Mrs Horsfall on Easter Monday in 1873

**77** Excitement in New Street one September da⟨y⟩ in 1865, when the foundation stone of the Mason⟨ic⟩ Hall was laid by Lord Leigh. (In the same year th⟨e⟩ cable of the first Atlantic Telegraph was made i⟨n⟩ Birmingham, 2,300 nautical miles long; the iro⟨n⟩ wire which formed the strand being about 16,00⟨0⟩ miles in length.)

78    Mr Matthews' Committee room in Nechells, 1892

Waiting in New Street for the visit of the Prince and Princess of Wales, when they came to open
ria Courts on 21 July 1891

**80**   Watching the laying of telephone wires in Colmore Row, June 1898

81 The Baden-Powell appeal for money for the women and children of Mafeking, 1900. The stand is manned in the photograph by the boys of King Edward's Grammar School

82 The Theatrical Charity Sports procession passing along Easy Row, 1902

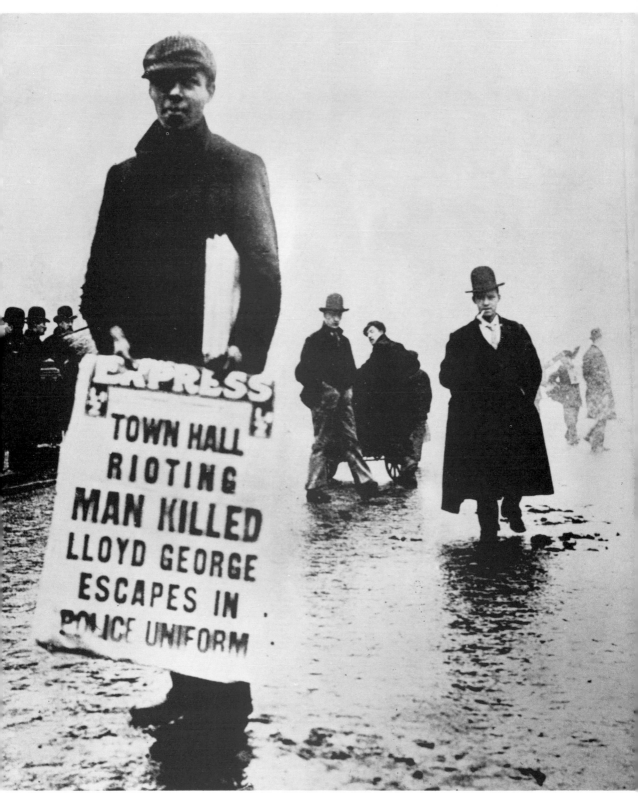

**83** How Birmingham and the Country at large heard about the escape of the famous politician from the Town Hall dressed in a policeman's uniform. Lloyd George was called the arch apostle of pro-Boerism. Birmingham people resented his appearance and violent scuffles ensued. The date was 18 December 1901

**84**  Primrose Day collection in Corporation Street, 19 April 1904. The photographer made a note on the back of the photograph that a record sale was made that year!

85    The Sheriff's carriage leaving the Law Courts during the March assizes, 1904

86    King Edward VII with Queen Alexandra opening the new Birmingham waterworks in the Elan Valley, 21 July 1904

87 *(overleaf)*    Birmingham City Council on a voyage of discovery: a visit to Elan Valley waterworks, 19 June 1900

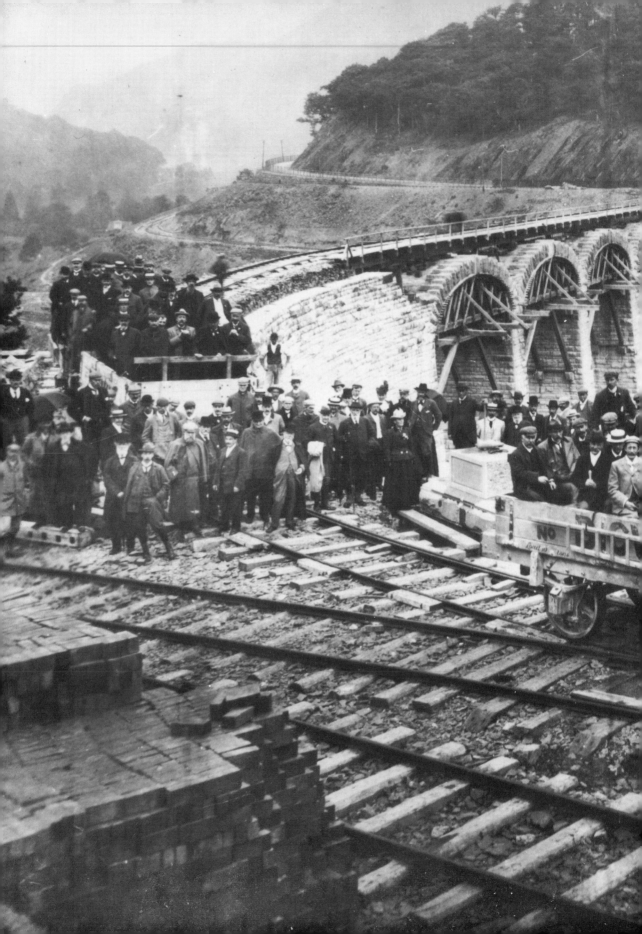

**88** A great man celebrates his birthday – this photograph shows Mr Joseph Chamberlain accompanied by Mrs Chamberlain, arriving for the Lord Mayor's reception and luncheon at the Council House on the eve of his seventieth birthday. The date was 7 July 1906

**89** Mr Joseph Chamberlain's birthday celebrations continue with a grand procession of motor-cars to Victoria Park, Small Heath and Ward End Park, July 1906

**90** A tram accident in Birmingham Lodge Road, 1 October 1907. A tram turned over as the brakes failed on the hill; many passengers were injured because in panic they jumped from the tram as it gathered momentum

**91** Scenes in Soho Road on the day when King Edward VII should have been crowned. The Coronation, which had been planned for 26 June 1902, had to be postponed because of the King's sudden illness. However, the cycle procession took place as originally intended, in the afternoon. King Edward was crowned on 9 August in the same year

**92** *(left)* On 7 July 1909, after a lunch which included 'Tartelettes de Caviar', King Edward VII and Queen Alexandra, accompanied by HRH Princess Victoria, with the Rt Hon R. B. Haldane, KC, MP, Minister in Attendance, set off down Hill Street on the way to open the University of Birmingham

**93** *(right)* The Water Department arch which was erected in Broad Street to celebrate the Royal visit in July 1909

**94** A view of the proceedings at the opening of the University of Birmingham, 1909

**96**   The cycle trade welcomes Their Majesties, 1909

*ft)*   Here is the Firemen's arch in Temple Row, July 1909

**97**  Life goes on beneath the decorations in Corporation Street, July 1909

**98**  An audience at the New Century picture theatre 1906, at Curzon Hall, which later became the West End cinema. The conductor of the orchestra is thought to be Joseph Engelmann, father of the late Franklin Engelmann

**99**  Dr W. J. Hall-Edwards, who was educated at King Edward's School, demonstrating the use of the X-Ray process to medicine, at Hodge Hill. This must have been one of the earliest photographs of the process taken

100　The opening of Ward End Park by Alderman Hallewell Rogers, 14 May 1904

# SOCIAL OCCASIONS

101  Taking the pets for a walk in South Road at the turn of the century

**102** The activities of Birmingham 1868 to 1869, preserved for all time by the contemporary camera of Sir Benjamin Stone

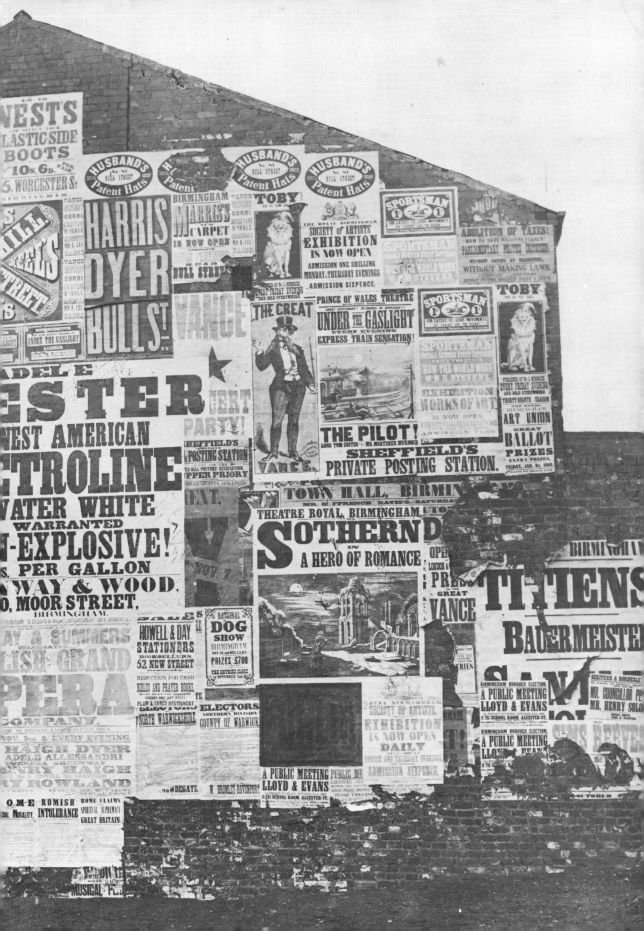

103   A mid-summer picnic party on the Avon. The time was 5 p.m., the date 14 June 1890

104   The Birmingham Loyal Volunteers, founded by Harry Gem in 1879

*At Sutton Park the volunteers*
*Having nimbly cut their capers*
*They shooted hooted drilled and swilled*
*And read the Pickwick Papers.*

**105** In the 'free and easy' of certain public houses, concert hall entertainment was born. This photograph (*c.* 1850) reveals the Old Rodney in Coleshill Street, transformed by Mr Holder into Holder's Concert Hall in 1846. The hall contained a splendid organ which was built by Hill of London. Could this be Mr Henry Holder in person waiting to greet his patrons? The dimensions of the room were 27 ft wide by 18 ft long. Fine ale and Dublin porter were on sale

**106**  A school party passing the Theatre Royal in New Street, 1902

**107** *(left)*  It has been said that the game of cricket was played in Birmingham in 1745 and the Birmingham Cricket Club merely re-established the game in 1818. Tradition has it that on the first day of play in 1818 a young lady looked up and said that she hoped that it would infuse some activity into the young men of Birmingham. Monument House, Edgbaston was the scene of many early games – every Tuesday at 3-0 p.m. One Marsden defended his wicket for four successive days, scoring between 400 and 500 runs (over-hand bowling was not then permitted). A verse of the period ran:

> Here lies Zal Smith wot is far away,
> Her wudner ha gone but her cudna stay
> Two zore legs and a baddish corf
> But the legs wor wot carried he horf.

Notable cricketers of the Victorian period in Birmingham included George Barker, George Holyoake, Henry Moore Griffiths, William James, S. A. Goddard, Samuel Beale, John Towers Laurence, John Bennett, and John Aston. The date or the identity of the players in the photograph has not been established, but it is possible that some of the above are here

108 A cricket match at the Grange, the home of Sir Benjamin Stone, July 1895 between the Grange and the Orphanage. The players, from left to right (*standing*): George Smart, Rev C. Bleiben, Dora, Robert, W. Bradbury, Sir Benjamin Stone, Norman, C. Henderson. *On the tree:* Oscar and A. Hickman. *On ground:* G. Foster, W. Arnott, H. Matthews.

109 The County Cricket Ground at Edgbaston shortly before 1899

110 Aston Villa F.C. 1886–7. *Standing, left to right:* F. Coulton, J. Warner, F. Dawson, Reserve, J. Simmonds. *Sitting, middle row:* R. Davies, A. Brown, A. Hunter, H. Vaughton, D. Hodgetts. *On ground:* H. Yates, J. Burton.

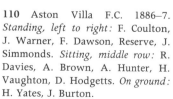

111　The rope-tying trick; a demonstration during lunch-time on waste ground in Corporation Street, near the Old Square, 1890

112, 113   George Bragg's wine cellars beneath the Theatre Royal, *c.* 1901

114    Exhibition time at Aston Lower Grounds, *c.* 1890

115    A sunny afternoon with the children in Cannon Hill park about 1900

116 Curling on Windley pool over the border in Sutton Coldfield in February 1895

117 An archaeological sightseeing expedition by members of the Vesey Club, c. 1899

# COUNTRY AND SUBURBS

**118**    Trotting along the Hagley Road and just passing the Plough and Harrow,
*c.* 1900

**119**  Once-peaceful Five Ways at the turn of the century

120    The garden of the old farm house in Edgbaston Lane, 1898

121    The Mill in the same Lane

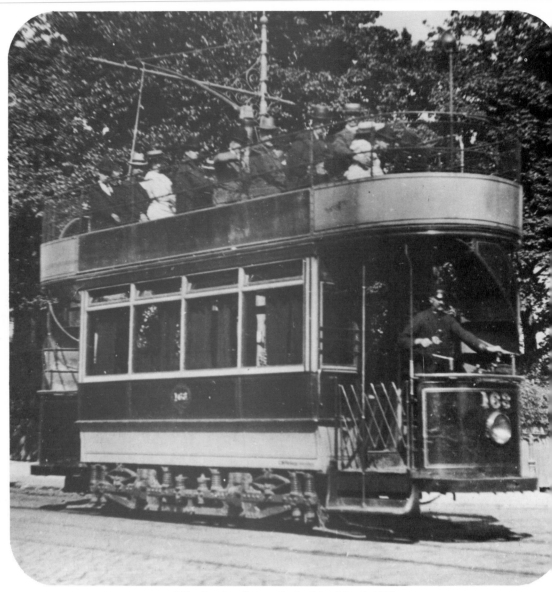

122    An electric tram in the Bristol Road, 1902

123 Mrs J. S. Nettlefold cutting the first sod of the Harborne Tenants Estate on Saturday 26 October 1907. In 1906 some enthusiasts for town planning realised that a 36 acre estate called Moor Pool was in danger of being spoiled by speculative builders. However, an option on the land was obtained by Councillor J. S. Nettlefold. As a result a meeting of enthusiasts who wished to provide good, well-built homes with gardens and yet to be within the means of workmen and artisans was held on 25 June 1907. The society thus formed was called The Harborne Tenants Limited

One of the homes on the borne Tenants Estate, c. 1909

May-day festivities with the ants of the Harborne Estate, May 0

126 The first employer to understand the importance of environment and in consequence to do something about it was George Cadbury. He dreamed of a perfect town in the country where workers could live in model houses surrounded by gardens. In 1879 he moved his business from Birmingham, where it had been since 1824, to ground between Griffin's brook and Bourn brook. Mr Cadbury built 143 homes for his workpeople which he sold at cost price. A lease of 999 years ensured that the gardens and vegetation would be preserved. Each house occupied only one quarter of the land alloted to it; the rest was garden

127 Layout of the workmen's cottages, Bournville, 1879

**128**  A Bournville parlour, *c.* 1895

BOURNVILLE

**129**  A space-saving measure: the tip-up bath in the kitchen, *c.* 1910

130  The home of Miss Brown on Hockley Hill, 1901

131 *(right)*  Hockley Brook in Factory Road, June 18

132 *(overleaf)*  The gipsy encampment on the Black Patch, Handsworth, 1

**133** The rope walk near Soho Road Station, 1898

**134** The old toll-gate at the corner of Hampstead Road and Villa Road, 1897

**135** When winter came to Terry Lane, Erdington, *c.* 1890

**136** Mrs Wimpress, house-keeper, beside the dove-cote outside Harry Greener's cottage, Grange Lane, Erdington, 1895

**137**  A winter morning at Mr Henry Fowler's farm, Holifast, Erdington in 1893

**138** *(overleaf)*  The rick fire that took place at the corner of Chester Road and Grange Lane, Erdington, on 31 July 1899

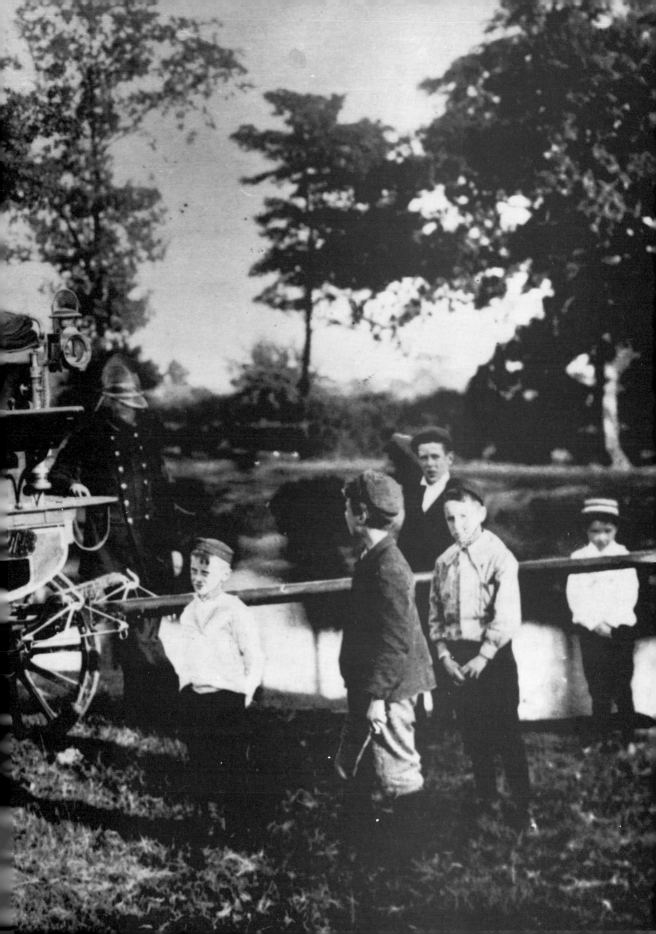

**139** A beautiful day for a trip to the Agricultural Show, Four Oaks, just outside the railway station. The day was 22 June 1898

140 Another load safely round the bend in Ebrook Lane, Pype Hayes, 1893

**141**   The mill and the miller at Castle Bromwich

**142**   A trip in mid-winter along the Stratford Road on a Sparkbrook steam tram. The building in the centre of the photograph is that of the well-known Birmingham photographer Thomas Lewis, who was responsible for this photograph and others in the book. The wires for the electric trams seem to have been placed in position – ready for the great take-over. This photograph was probably taken on the last day of steam, 31 December 1906

**143** *(right)*   Track laying along the Stratford Road just at the junction of Farm Road, 190

**144** A suburban horse-bus waiting for passengers. The date is *c.* 1900

145 The Green, Moseley Village, when Mr Elliott the florist lived next door to George Clements, the landlord of the Bull's Head, 1873

146 The village has become a suburb

147  The cart horse of the local builder wears summer head gear, July 1901

148  A steam tram on the way to King's Heath, *c.* 1903